W9-BID-926

You Can Help

Jennifer B. Gillis

Rourke

Publishing LLC
Vero Beach, Florida 32964

www.rourkepublishing.com

PHOTO CREDITS: © Christian Carroll: cover

Editor: Robert Stengard-Olliges

Cover design by Nicola Stratford

Library of Congress Cataloging-in-Publication Data

Gillis, Jennifer Blizin, 1950-
  You can help! / Jennifer B. Gillis.
    p. cm. -- (My neighborhood)
  Includes index.
  ISBN 1-60044-206-4 (hardcover)
  ISBN 1-59515-556-2 (softcover)
  1. Community life--Juvenile literature. 2. Social action--Juvenile literature. I. Title.
  HM761.G5553 2007
  307.3'362--dc22
                                2006022171

Printed in the USA

CG/CG

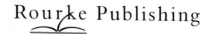

Rourke Publishing

www.rourkepublishing.com – sales@rourkepublishing.com
Post Office Box 3328, Vero Beach, FL 32964
1-800-394-7055

Table of Contents

Your Community   4

Being Responsible   6

Showing Respect   8

Community Resources   10

Keep it Clean!   12

Keep it Safe!   14

Being Fair   16

Being Kind   18

Sharing   20

It's Up to You!   22

Glossary   23

Index   24

Your Community

Your **community** is where you live. Houses, buildings, and parks are in your community.

People are in your community, too. You can help them make your community better.

Being Responsible

Your community belongs to you. You can help take care of it.

Take time to help out. That is being **responsible**.

Showing Respect

Respect means showing that you care. You can respect places in your community.

You can respect people in your community, too.
Always follow the rules.

Community Resources

A **resource** is something all people can use. A place can be a community resource.

Things can be community resources, too. Take care
of them so they last a long time.

Keep it Clean!

You can help keep your community clean. **Recycle** cans, paper, and glass.

Pick up trash, even if it isn't yours.

Keep it Safe!

Be responsible about safety. Play in a safe area.

Ask an adult for help if you don't feel safe. This girl
is asking for directions.

Being Fair

Being fair means treating everyone the same. Let everyone have a turn.

Give everyone a chance. Welcome new people to your community.

Being Kind

Being kind means thinking about others. You can do things for people who need help.

Think about how you want to be treated. Then, act that way to others.

Sharing

You can share with your friends. Make sure everyone has a little bit.

You can share with your community, too. Make sure everyone has the things they need.

It's Up to You!

Everyone is part of a community. What people do makes a difference to others. You are an important part of your community. How will you show it?

GLOSSARY

community (kuh MYOO nuh tee) — group of people or place where group of people live

recycle (ree SYE kuhl) — to put things like cans, bottles, and paper in special containers so that they can be treated and used again

resource (REE sorss) — a place or thing that can be used by many people

responsible (ri SPON suh buhl) — to act in a way that shows you care for something

INDEX

fairness   16

houses   4

kindness   18

parks   4

recycling   12

respect   8, 9

rules   9

safety   14

sharing   20, 21

trash   13

FURTHER READING

Cole, Joanna. *Sharing is Fun.* Harper Collins, 2004.

Ganeri, Anita. *Something Old, Something New: Recycling.* Heinemann, 2005.

Hennessy, B.G. *Because of You: A Book of Kindness*. Candlewick Press, 2005.

WEBSITES TO VISIT

www.epa.gov/reyclecity

www.charactercounts.org

ABOUT THE AUTHOR

Jennifer B. Gillis is an author and editor of nonfiction books and poetry for children. A graduate of Gilford College in North Carolina, she has taught foreign language and social studies in North Carolina, Virginia, and Illinois.